This is a fictionalised biography describing some of the key moments (so far!) in the career of Neymar.

Some of the events described in this book are based upon the author's imagination and are probably not entirely accurate representations of what actually happened.

Tales from the Pitch
Neymar
by Matt Carver

Published by Raven Books
An imprint of Ransom Publishing Ltd.
Unit 7, Brocklands Farm, West Meon, Hampshire GU32 1JN, UK
www.ransom.co.uk

ISBN   978 180047 691 2
First published in 2023

Copyright © 2023 Ransom Publishing Ltd.
Text copyright © 2023 Ransom Publishing Ltd.
Cover illustration by Ben Farr © 2023 Ben Farr

A CIP catalogue record of this book is available from the British Library.

All rights reserved. No part of this publication may be reproduced, stored in a retrieval system, or transmitted, in any form or by any means, electronic, mechanical, photocopying, recording or otherwise, without the prior permission of the publishers.

The rights of Matt Carver to be identified as the author and of Ben Farr to be identified as the illustrator of this Work have been asserted by them in accordance with sections 77 and 78 of the Copyright, Design and Patents Act 1988.

TALES FROM THE PITCH

NEYMAR

MATT CARVER

RAVEN

To Danielle and Olive,
for equal parts encouragement and distraction

CONTENTS

		Page
1	Impossible	7
2	Neymar Júnior	14
3	Keeping Up with the Neymars	18
4	Futsal	22
5	Santos	27
6	Spain, Part One	33
7	Professional	40
8	Flair Play	45
9	The New Prince	51
10	Spain, Part Two	58
11	Golden	63
12	Six Minutes	69
13	Champions	78
14	Redemption	84
15	To Move or Not to Move	91
16	Déjà Vu	96
17	Agony	103
18	Friends Reunited	110
19	Legend	114

1
IMPOSSIBLE

March 2017, Camp Nou, Barcelona, Spain
Champions League Last-16 2nd Leg, Barcelona v PSG

Neymar sat in silence as he laced up his boots. This wasn't the usual way he prepared for a game – normally he'd be bouncing around the dressing room, joking with his team-mates. But this game was different.

Three weeks ago, Barcelona had lost 4-0 in Paris, to Paris Saint-Germain, in the first leg of the Champions League last-16. Barca had been comfortably beaten, with Ángel Di María stealing the show for PSG with a stunning brace.

Barcelona would now have to win the return leg by five goals to go through to the next round – or score four and then go on to win the dreaded penalty shootout.

Neymar thought back to the Instagram post he'd made after the first leg, when he'd told his followers, "While there is a 1% chance, we will have 99% faith."

Even now, just before the game, he didn't really think it was possible to come back and win.

"OK, guys. We all know this isn't going to be easy," Barca captain Andrés Iniesta announced, looking around at his team-mates. "But today we are at home – we have the crowd behind us."

He paused, making sure that the players were all listening. "Don't worry about the first leg. Just go out and show the world what we can do. We've got MSN – Messi, Suárez and Neymar – after all!"

Neymar looked at the two players sitting either side of him in the dressing room. Lionel Messi and Luis Suárez – two of the best players in the world.

With me, three of the best, Neymar thought.

As the teams lined up in the tunnel, Neymar looked across at the PSG players. He could see Thiago Silva, Marquinhos and Lucas Moura joking with each other. They were Brazil team-mates of his, but now, when they looked across at him, he ignored them and just stared straight ahead.

Moments later, the game kicked off, with the last notes of the Champions League anthem, mixed with the roars of the crowd, still ringing in Neymar's ears.

Only three minutes in, Suárez opened the scoring. After a scrappy clearance, he beat the keeper to the ball, and his header just about snuck over the line.

GOAL! 1-0 to Barcelona. Four more goals to go.

The Barca fans in the Nou Camp were already in great voice. The atmosphere had been deafening before kick-off – now it ramped up another notch. Neymar knew that the Barca fans would make all the difference – they were an essential part of Barcelona's fightback.

A few minutes later, Neymar had his first chance. He cut inside onto his right foot and curled a shot narrowly wide.

"So close! Keep going!" Messi called over to him

encouragingly. Neymar rubbed the back of his head in frustration.

There were no goals in the next 20 minutes, and Neymar was beginning to wonder whether Barca would have enough time to get the goals they needed.

Just then, Suárez played the ball forward to meet the run of Iniesta, who managed to backheel it across the face of the PSG goal.

The PSG defender, Layvin Kurzawa, tried to kick the ball clear, but only managed to slice it into the back of his own goal.

2-0 to Barcelona on the night!

Neymar picked the ball out of the net and ran with it back to the centre circle.

"Come on, we can do this!" he yelled to his team-mates.

As the half-time whistle blew, the players left the pitch to the chorus of "el Himne Del Barça" – Barcelona's famous chant – echoing around the Nou Camp. PSG were struggling in the hostile atmosphere and the Barcelona players knew it.

In the dressing room, the Barca manager, Luis Enrique,

spoke to each of the players individually, and eventually came to Neymar.

"You're doing great, Ney – you've got them worried. They're nervous now. Just keep showing them what you can do – you don't need to change anything."

Just after kick-off, Neymar chased a loose ball into the PSG penalty area. The defender slipped and crashed head-first into Neymar's legs, knocking him to the floor. It was a no-brainer, and the ref pointed to the penalty spot.

Messi stepped forward and calmly smashed the ball home.

THAT WAS THREE!

Neymar ruffled Messi's hair in delight as they ran back to the centre circle. He was determined to keep up the momentum. Now it was only 4-3 to PSG on aggregate.

But then, soon after, disaster struck. A long PSG ball forward was headed down to the edge of the area, and their deadly Uruguayan striker, Edinson Cavani, fired home.

This was bad news for Barca. This was an away goal, so Barca could no longer draw and go to penalties. Now they needed to win by five clear goals. With only 30 minutes left, they needed three more.

With just five minutes of normal time left, it looked as if it was all over. Then Barcelona won a free kick on the edge of the area. Neymar pulled up his socks, and coolly curled the ball into the top corner.

FOUR!

He was delighted with such a great goal, but there was no time to celebrate. Five minutes left, with Barcelona needing two more goals.

Just a minute later, Suárez was tripped by a defender in the box, and Barcelona had another penalty.

This time Messi let Neymar take it.

"You can do it," Messi said confidently, as Neymar walked past him to the spot.

He was right. Neymar opened up his body and placed the ball into the bottom corner.

FIVE!

The Barca fans couldn't believe what they were witnessing. One more goal. Could they really do this?

Then, with only 30 seconds of injury time left, Neymar dropped deep to get on the ball.

Spotting Sergi Roberto running past the PSG defenders, he floated a perfect cross towards him. Neymar held his breath as Roberto stretched and managed to get a toe to the ball, prodding it past the keeper.

6-1 to Barcelona! They'd done it – with only seconds to spare.

Moments later, the full-time whistle went, and the Barcelona players all ran into the centre circle to celebrate together. They'd achieved the impossible, largely thanks to the magic of Neymar.

"We couldn't have done it without you!" Luis Enrique yelled, his arms around Neymar's shoulders.

Neymar felt on top of the world. This was one of the best performances of his life, and one of the most important games in which to achieve it.

Later, as Neymar was walking back to the dressing room, the president of PSG, Nasser Al-Khelaifi, walked over to him.

"Even though we lost, you were amazing to watch," he said graciously. "Maybe one day we will see you play like that for PSG."

2
NEYMAR JÚNIOR

June 1992, Mogi das Cruzes, São Paulo, Brazil

"Have you strapped him in, Nadine?" Neymar Senior asked his wife. Neymar Júnior was in the child seat in the back of the car, kicking his feet excitedly. He was only four months old.

"Of course I have. Now get in and drive," Nadine replied impatiently.

Neymar Senior climbed gingerly into the driver's seat

of the car. His legs were still aching. That morning he'd been playing for União Mogi FC and he'd been on the receiving end of some rough tackles.

The roads were slick with rain as they began to drive south, out of the city, on the way to visit Neymar Júnior's grandparents in São Vicente.

"I'm going to take the mountain road," said Neymar Senior. "This time of day, the roads through the city are going to be full of traffic."

"Just be careful in this weather." Nadine smiled, looking back at Júnior, who was now peacefully asleep despite the rain hammering on the windows.

The car crept slowly up the road, approaching a waterfall on a sharp bend. As they turned the corner, a car came hurtling towards them on the wrong side of the road.

Before they had time to react, the approaching car slammed into Neymar Senior's door, forcing them off the road and into the waterfall.

"Júnior!" Nadine cried out instinctively. She looked around, but couldn't see Neymar Júnior anywhere. His child seat was empty.

She turned in panic to Neymar Senior, who was moaning in pain.

"I can't move, Nadine. My legs … " he said faintly, pointing at his twisted hips. "You'll need to get help. I don't know if I'll make it."

Nadine crawled out of her seat and through the shattered rear windscreen, then waved and shouted at passing cars.

Soon, a van stopped and two men ran over to help.

"Call an ambulance, now!" one of the men said to the other, as soon as they saw Neymar Senior, mangled and trapped under his seat belt.

"Forget the ambulance! Just find my baby boy!" Neymar Senior yelled.

One of the men climbed through the smashed window into the car and, seconds later, pulled out a small bundle, crying loudly.

It was Neymar Júnior.

Frantic, Nadine ran over to her son. The baby's clothes had blood on them, but he was alive.

As soon as the ambulance arrived, one of the paramedics checked Júnior over.

"It's just a cut," he said. "Probably from the broken glass – he's going to be fine."

Nadine sighed with relief.

Neymar Senior wasn't so lucky. They had to cut him out of the car, and he was rushed to hospital with a dislocated hip.

The next day, when Nadine and Júnior visited him in hospital, Neymar Senior looked despondent.

"I don't think I'm going to be able to play football again."

"How can you think about football at a time like this?" Nadine exclaimed. "Just thank God we are all safe and alive!"

"Maybe Júnior can pick up where I left off," Neymar Senior said, as he smiled at his son, nestled in Nadine's arms.

Neymar Júnior smiled back.

3
KEEPING UP WITH THE NEYMARS

March 1997, São Vicente, São Paulo, Brazil

Neymar Júnior ran down the street, chasing the ball as quickly as he could. He felt a shove in his back, then fell to the floor, scuffing his clothes.

"Hey, he's only a little kid! Go easy!" Neymar's team-mate, Gabriel, shouted.

"If he plays with us, he gets treated just like everyone else," the older boy who'd pushed him replied casually.

"Well, that's a free-kick anyway," said Gabriel.

Neymar stood up and dusted himself off. "Can I take it?" he asked nervously.

"Sure, kid – knock yourself out. You're the one who was fouled," Gabriel grinned.

Five-year-old Neymar stood behind the ball. It almost reached his knees. He looked up at the "goal" – a couple of white lines painted on the side of a garage.

The older boy stood in front of him, making a wall. Another boy stood in goal.

Neymar ran up to the ball and swung his leg, as if he was going to kick it as hard as he could. The "wall" jumped high, and the keeper threw himself to his left, anticipating the shot.

Instead, Neymar feinted and cheekily rolled the ball along the floor, into the bottom corner of the "goal".

"Goal!" Arms outstretched, he wheeled away in celebration. His team-mates joined him, laughing at Neymar's audacity.

The other team looked on angrily, furious at being embarrassed so easily by a five-year-old kid.

Just then, Neymar heard the nearby church bells

ringing for midday. He needed to be home for his little sister's first birthday celebration.

"Got to go!" he called out, as he dashed off, leaving the rest of the players standing and watching him disappear.

The family apartment was nearby. Neymar lived there with his parents, his grandparents and his baby sister. His grandparents had moved in with them after his sister was born, as they didn't have enough money for their own home.

Neymar rushed in, his face flushed from running, and his clothes still covered in dust.

"Júnior! Quickly!" His mother fussed around him, brushing his hair and straightening his dusty clothes.

Neymar walked into the bedroom and saw his sister, Rafaella, sitting on their grandmother's lap. She was scowling, and her grandparents were trying to amuse her with a pink toy elephant.

Rafaella looked up, saw Neymar and started giggling.

"What are you laughing at?" Neymar chuckled, grabbing Rafaella and giving her a cuddle. He could always make her smile. "Happy birthday, little sister!"

The family sat and shared out a birthday cake,

although Rafaella managed to get more cake on her face than in her mouth. The only person who was missing was Neymar Senior.

"Where's Dad?" Neymar asked in a quiet moment.

"He managed to pick up another shift at work – he couldn't turn it down," his mother replied sadly.

Since his football career had come to an early end, Neymar's father had been working three jobs, but he still wasn't making enough money for them to be comfortable.

Neymar Senior arrived home later that evening, after Rafaella had fallen asleep in the shared family bedroom. The rest of the family sat quietly in the kitchen, not wanting to wake her after the day's excitement.

"Hey Júnior," said his father with a grin, "how about we go for a quick kick-about before bed?"

The pair went outside in the fading light, and Neymar showed his dad how he'd scored the free-kick against the older boys. Neymar Senior laughed and pulled his son close.

"You'll always be playing with someone older or bigger than you," he told him. "But that just means you have to be the sharpest and smartest player out there!"

4
FUTSAL

February 1999, São Vicente, São Paulo, Brazil

Neymar Senior weaved around two players on the beach court, before firing the ball past the goalkeeper and into the net.

Watching from the stands, Neymar Júnior and his mum jumped up in celebration.

Neymar Senior didn't get much chance to play any more and, when he did, his hip often gave him trouble.

The family were always very supportive when he played, knowing that these opportunities didn't last forever.

Today was no exception and, as the pain in his hip grew worse, he was soon substituted. He sat on the bench and placed an ice pack on his hip, then gave Júnior and Nadine a thumbs-up.

Without his dad playing, Neymar Júnior quickly lost interest in the game, and began doing tricks with a small ball he'd brought with him.

He juggled the ball, keeping it off the ground as he flicked it from foot to foot. A small group of children gathered around him, watching in awe.

"No way!" they cried out, as he caught the ball on the back of his neck, before letting it roll down his chest and resuming keepie-ups.

A little further along the beach, Betinho dos Santos, a scout for the famous local club, Santos, was watching the games on the beach. A couple of years ago, he'd discovered and signed the latest wonderkid to Santos. Now he was searching for his next success story.

Nobody on the beach had caught his attention, but

then he heard the cries of the children watching a little kid doing keepie-ups.

The scout began watching, and within seconds he knew he'd found what he was looking for.

Betinho strolled over to a group of adults who were watching, and spoke to Nadine. "Is that your son?" he asked.

She nodded nervously.

"He's very good! Really talented for his age." Betinho paused, then added, "I'm a scout for the club, Santos. I'd love to see your son on a futsal court."

Nadine didn't know much about futsal, other than that it was a smaller, indoor version of football.

"I'll ask his father, and bring him along if we can," she replied, thinking that giving Neymar Júnior an outlet that kept him busy and safe would be a good thing.

Two weeks later, Neymar Júnior and his father walked into the courts at the local futsal club, Portuguesa Santista.

As Neymar Senior walked over to Betinho, Neymar watched the boys training. Many were older than him, and they were playing a five-a-side practice match on a small pitch in the hall.

Immediately, Neymar felt at home. This was like the street football that he was used to, just with rules and a referee. And, even better, there was a round ball and flat ground to play on.

The play was fast and technical, with each player only a having a few seconds (and a few yards) with the ball to make an impact.

"What do you think, Júnior?" his father asked, as he and Betinho came over to him.

"I want to play *now*," Neymar replied. "Do you have any kit and some boots I can use?"

The two men laughed.

"He's keen!" said Betinho. "Why don't I give him a quick trial?"

They found a shirt for Neymar. It was the smallest they had, but it was still too big.

Betinho had a quiet word with one of the coaches, who signalled for Neymar to join in.

As play resumed, Neymar immediately demanded the ball. "Pass to me, to me!"

Another boy slid the ball over to him.

Neymar looked up and saw a defender approaching. He did three step-overs and, as the boy moved forward, slipped the ball to the side and danced past him.

Another defender came across, and Neymar checked inside, before drilling the ball past the keeper, into the goal.

He turned around, expecting a few cheers of celebration. Instead, everyone just stood in stunned silence.

Betinho smiled at Neymar Senior.

"I think he'll fit in just fine."

5
SANTOS

May 2003, Vila Belmiro, Santos, Brazil

Portuguesa Santista were losing. With only five minutes left of the semi-final, they were 3-1 down.

This was the first time in the São Paulo regional futsal tournament that Santista had been behind – and Neymar was feeling the pressure that came with being his team's star player.

After his trial four years ago, he'd been offered a place

in the Portuguesa Santista team. Betinho had known straight away that Neymar would be the best player in the team – and he'd been right. Neymar was in a league of his own, and his team turned to him for inspiration.

Now, 3-1 down, time was running out – and his team-mates were struggling to create chances. Neymar dropped deeper in search of the ball, desperate to make an impact.

"Come on, Neymar! We need some more of your magic here," one of his team-mates shouted.

"I'm trying!" he yelled back, as another ambitious pass was cut out by the opposition defence.

Again, Neymar fell back, picking up the ball from his keeper. He burst forward, before fizzing it across to a team-mate.

As the ball was laid back to him, Neymar blazed it high into the top corner of the goal.

GOAL! Santista were back in the game. They were now 3-2 down, with only seconds of normal time remaining.

As his team-mates celebrated, Neymar urgently beckoned them back for kick-off. They weren't done yet.

Play resumed and Neymar went on a mazy dribble, beating two defenders down the left wing.

Looking up, he spotted a team-mate unmarked in the box. He flashed a perfect pass, but the shot that followed was high and wide. Neymar was careful to hide his disappointment.

"That was so close. Keep going!" he called out.

Moments later, the final whistle went and Neymar slumped to the ground, devastated. They'd been knocked out at the semi-final stage. He looked up at the stands and saw his parents proudly applauding.

At half-time, his dad had told him that scouts from the big local clubs were watching the game. Neymar had seen the badges on the tracksuits, from São Paulo, Corinthians and Palmeiras, but he hadn't really paid much attention.

"I'm sorry, Dad," he said, as he joined his parents in the stands. "We didn't even make it to the final. I bet none of the scouts will be interested now."

"Nonsense, Júnior – we all know you were the best player out there. But football is a team sport. Sometimes the best player isn't on the winning team."

As they sat together and watched the remaining matches, Betinho and another Santos scout came over to the family.

"I'm Zito," the other scout said, introducing himself. "That was an impressive performance, young man," he said to Neymar.

"I know exactly who you are – you were my father's favourite player!" Neymar said, jumping up excitedly.

"This man won the World Cup – twice!" Neymar Senior said, turning to his son.

"That was a long time ago now!" Zito laughed. "And I think your son could be a better player than I ever was!"

Neymar just stood there, not sure how to respond.

"We'd love to sign you for Santos," Betinho told Neymar. "But unfortunately you're still too young – we don't have a youth team for your age."

"Then we'll create a team for him!" exclaimed Zito. "We'll make an Under-11 team just for him. We've got to bring that kid here."

Neymar looked to his father, who nodded enthusiastically.

"Yes please," said Neymar with a grin, "I'd like that very much."

A few days later, Neymar was back at the Vila Belmiro stadium, home of Santos FC. He was there with his parents, to sign the contract confirming that he was joining the club.

A photographer clicked away as they shook hands with lots of men in suits.

"Would you like a proper tour?" Zito asked Neymar. Zito had quietly slipped in at the back of the room – Neymar had only noticed him because he was the only one wearing a tracksuit.

Excited, Neymar nodded and followed Zito out of the meeting room and along a corridor.

Zito ushered him through a small door, and Neymar suddenly realised he was standing in the players' tunnel.

He looked along the tunnel and saw the flash of the green pitch, bathed in bright sunlight.

"One day you'll be lined up here," said Zito quietly.

"I hope so," said Neymar politely. He didn't want to

appear overconfident, especially when he was standing next to a World Cup winner – but playing for Santos was exactly what he was going to do.

Next, Zito took him to the club museum – the Memorial das Conquistas. Neymar gazed in wonder at trophy after trophy, next to old black-and-white photos of players he didn't recognise.

"I know who this is!" he cried out suddenly, when he came to a section dedicated to Pelé.

"Ah yes, Pelé – the King," Zito grinned. "We played together, you know. I probably owe both of my World Cup medals to him. He was the best – for Santos and for Brazil. Nobody will ever match what he achieved."

Neymar stared at a picture of Pelé. He was sitting on his team-mate's shoulders and was clenching his fist in celebration.

Neymar didn't want to say anything out loud, but the thought came to him immediately.

Maybe, one day, I will match what he achieved.

6
SPAIN, PART ONE

February 2006, Santiago Bernabéu, Madrid, Spain

As the Real Madrid players ran out onto the pitch, the Los Blancos fans roared in support.

Neymar Senior turned to speak to his son, but his words were drowned out by the crowd.

The pair were sitting high up in the director's box but, even from there, Neymar could feel the enormous energy of 80,000 fans chanting and cheering.

Three years had passed since Neymar had signed for Santos. As part of their youth system, he'd developed hugely as a player – honing his skills as a fast and skilful winger with an eye for goal.

His growing reputation had caught the attention of Spanish giants Real Madrid, and they'd contacted his father, asking if Neymar would spend a few weeks with them.

The answer was obvious and, after arriving in Madrid, Neymar had been training with their under-16s team.

The level of football was much higher than he was used to at Santos, but Neymar was eager to show he was up to the challenge.

Today, as a break from training, the coaches had suggested he watch the first-team play in their Copa del Rey match.

Now, in the Bernabéu, Neymar could experience the highest level of European football – and get a taste for what professional football might hold for him.

As the players lined up to shake hands, the noise died down enough for Neymar to hear what his father was saying.

"Here they are – the Galácticos, the superstars. I'll point them out for you, Júnior," he said, bending down towards his son.

"That's Ronaldo – the phenomenon. Watch him closely – his movement is incredible. And that's Roberto Carlos – see how much he gets up and down the left wing, and how powerful his shot is!"

Neymar gazed down at the players – the best in the world. What would it feel like to be down there, to be one of them?

"The other Brazilians are Júlio Baptista and Cicinho, both top players," his dad added. "And don't forget about Zinedine Zidane and David Beckham. Los Galácticos."

Suddenly, Santos and the Vila Belmiro felt a long way away. Neymar was used to the relaxed atmosphere of a small stadium. But this was serious.

The game kicked off and, less than a minute in, the ball broke loose on the edge of the opposition penalty area. The right-back, Cicinho, burst forward and blazed a shot into the top corner.

Neymar jumped up in excitement.

"Did you see that?" he called out.

"Amazing!" his dad replied. "These players are the real deal, Júnior."

Just three minutes later, Beckham whipped a cross in from the right wing.

The ball flew past the desperate defenders and found its way to Ronaldo, in the far corner of the box.

Taking it first time, he swept the ball under the keeper for another goal. In the blink of an eye, Los Blancos were 2-0 up.

Straight after the restart, Beckham curled another pinpoint cross into the box.

With one more touch, the defender was beaten and the ball was in the net.

"Three-nil in less than ten minutes!" Neymar Senior shouted to his son. "What do you think, Júnior? Do you fancy playing here?"

Neymar just sat open-mouthed, in stunned silence.

At half-time, one of the youth-team coaches walked over to them.

"I've arranged for you to meet the players after the game," he said to young Neymar with a grin. "They should be able to tell you what it's really like to play for Real Madrid!"

Once more, Neymar's mouth dropped open.

Fifteen minutes into the second-half, Real Madrid won a free-kick on the edge of the box.

Roberto Carlos laid the ball to Zidane, who tapped it back to him. Checking inside onto his left foot, he rocketed the ball into the far corner of the goal.

"And he's supposed to be a defender!" laughed Neymar Senior.

The game finished 4-0 to Real Madrid – and Neymar was awestruck by the quality of the Real Madrid players. He just could not believe how good they were.

The coach quickly ushered Neymar down the stairs and over to the entrance to the Real Madrid dressing room.

As he opened the door, Neymar found himself face-to-face with the Real players, all laughing and talking, celebrating the win.

He was directed over to a corner of the room, where he could see seats with names and numbers above them. *Baptista – 8. Ronaldo – 9. Cicinho – 11.*

"Hey, kid! I hear you're going to be the next superstar!" Ronaldo called out.

Neymar smiled shyly. "I'm not as good as you guys – that was amazing!" he replied.

"Well, we try!" Ronaldo grinned.

"You're from Santos, right?" Baptista asked. Like Neymar, Baptista was from Sao Paulo. "Do you know a guy named Betinho dos Santos?"

"I do!" replied Neymar. "He's the guy who asked me to join Santos in the first place."

"Well, he definitely knows a good player when he sees one," Baptista said, winking at Neymar.

"So, you think you want to join Real?" Roberto Carlos asked the youngster. "How old are you?"

"I'm fourteen – just!" Neymar replied. "And I'm not sure yet."

"Honestly, kid, I would stay where you are for now. Real Madrid want to buy stars, and Santos is one of the best places to become a star," Baptista said, suddenly looking serious.

Neymar trained with the Real Madrid youth team for a few more days, and then his trial came to an end.

After his last training session, Neymar's dad rushed over to him.

"They want to sign you, Júnior! They've offered you a deal to come and play here," he said, unable to hide his excitement. "Well done! I'm so proud of you. The biggest team in the world wants to sign my son!"

He beamed with pride.

"Does that mean Santos want me to leave?" Neymar asked.

"Of course not!" his dad replied. "I've actually spoken to Zito and, if you stay with them, Santos will give us a house near the stadium."

Neymar Senior paused and looked at his son, knowing how important this decision was. "So, what will it be – Santos or Real Madrid? It's up to you, Júnior."

But Neymar had already made up his mind.

"I think I want to go home," he said quietly.

7
PROFESSIONAL

March 2009, Estádio do Pacaembu, São Paulo, Brazil
Campeonato Paulista, Santos v Oeste

The Santos manager, Vagner Mancini, turned to Neymar on the bench. "Can you hear that, lad? They're calling your name – you'd better go and get warmed up!"

Neymar turned to look at the Santos fans, who were loudly chanting his name. They'd all heard stories and seen YouTube videos of him in action for the Santos youth teams. They all knew that he was Santos' rising star. Now they were desperate to see what he could do in the first-team.

Neymar jumped out of his seat, pleased to be able to channel his nervous energy into doing warm-ups.

Last month, on his 17th birthday, he'd signed his first professional contract – with Santos.

Since then, he'd been on the team sheet for every game, but he was yet to get off the bench.

Today, the crowd was restless. Santos were playing in the regional São Paulo state league, a local competition held in advance of the national league, later in the year.

They were expected to win most matches but, today, against Oeste, it was still 0-0, with almost an hour gone.

"You're going on, Neymar," Mancini told him, putting an arm around his shoulder. "Go out there and enjoy it. Don't worry about the nerves – everyone gets them. Just make sure you show the fans what we all know you can do."

Neymar was subbed on in the 59th minute, slotting into his familiar position on the right wing and replacing the Colombian international, Mauricio Molina.

Despite what Mancini had said to him, Neymar was anxious. This was his big chance, and he was playing alongside high quality players.

Was he really good enough to be playing in the first team? No doubt he was going to find out.

Less than a minute later, he picked up the ball to the right of the penalty area. He drove at the defender, before jinking to the right and darting past him. As another defender came across, he looped a dipping shot over the keeper, towards the far corner of the goal.

Agonisingly, it crashed against the bar – and was desperately scrambled away by the Oeste defence.

Time after time, he ran at the defenders and, before long, they started backing off, recognising that he was too fast and too skilful for them to mark tightly.

Shortly afterwards, the former Brazil international, Rôni, put Santos ahead, and they went on to win the game 2-1.

As they walked off the pitch, some of the Oeste players approached Neymar.

"Fancy swapping shirts?" one of them asked. "I reckon yours might be a bit special in a few years' time."

"I've already promised it to my dad," Neymar replied. "I think he's going to frame it."

The following week, Santos were at home to Paulista. Again, Neymar was subbed on in the second half and again, he didn't manage to score.

Playing at the Vila Belmiro had been a dream since he'd first signed for Santos, but today Neymar was too focused on making an impact to appreciate it.

The following week, after a long training session, Rôni pulled Neymar aside.

"You know your goal will come, don't you? You have to *believe* it will, not just *hope*," he said reassuringly. "It's the life of a forward, trying to find and keep that confidence," he added. "Trust me, I've been there."

"There's so much expectation," said Neymar. "The crowd are already chanting my name. I just want to prove how good I am."

"And you will. They only chant because they know how good you are – they just need to see you prove it."

The following game was back at the Estádio do

Pacaembu, against Mogi Mirim. This time, Neymar was starting – his first professional start.

Once more, he was playing on the right wing, with Rôni up front and one of Neymar's friends from the youth teams, Paulo Henrique Ganso, in centre-midfield.

And early in the second half, it was Ganso who gave Santos the lead, scoring from close range after a deflection.

When Rôni rose and powered in a header shortly after, Neymar started to think that, once more, it wouldn't be his day.

Then, just three minutes later, Neymar drifted inside from the right wing, as Rôni collected the ball on the left side of the box. Neymar anticipated the cross and got ahead of his marker, squirming free as the defender tried to grab his shirt.

The cross was perfect, and Neymar only had to stoop slightly to head the ball in from six yards out.

As the Santos fans celebrated, he punched the air with relief and satisfaction.

With a goal in his first professional start, he had finally arrived.

8
FLAIR PLAY

August 2010, Meadowlands Stadium, New Jersey, USA
International Friendly, USA v Brazil

"You should have gone to the World Cup," Dani Alves told Neymar glumly. "We might have done a bit better with you there."

They were sitting in the dressing room, just before kick-off, in Brazil's first friendly after the World Cup.

In just the previous month, Brazil had been knocked out in the quarter-finals of the World Cup, in South

Africa, losing 2-1 to the Netherlands. This wasn't supposed to happen to Brazil.

Neymar hadn't been called up for the World Cup squad but, perhaps recognising that mistake, Brazil had called him up for their very next fixture.

His Santos team-mate and old friend, Ganso, had joined him, also for his first international cap.

"Well, I'm sorry I wasn't there to help you then. But at least I can rescue you from now on!" Neymar told Dani Alves with a grin. In response, Dani Alves just picked up a balled-up sock and threw it at Neymar.

Following an impressive first year-and-a-half as a professional player, Neymar was rapidly growing in confidence. After his debut appearances in the Paulista state league, he'd also gone on to perform well in the Brazilian national league, the Série A.

And then, at the start of the 2010 season, his game had really taken off. Santos had won the Paulista, and Neymar had been their star player.

Santos had also won the Copa do Brasil, the Brazilian national cup, with Neymar ending as the tournament's top scorer.

"They said 14,000 people signed a petition for Neymar to play in this game," Ganso shouted across the dressing room to his team-mates.

"Thirteen thousand were probably just his dad, using different names!" Dani Alves grinned.

Now it was Neymar's turn to throw a sock.

The Brazil manager, Mano Menezes, called for the team's attention. "I love the confidence, lads. Make sure I see that confidence on the pitch too."

He paused and looked around the dressing room. "This is my first game as Brazil manager," he continued, "and for many of you, it's your first Brazil game too. It may only be a friendly, but this is the start of a new generation – so let's go out and show the fans that Brazil are back!"

As Neymar stood proudly on the pitch for the national anthems, he looked at the Brazil players standing alongside him.

To his right stood Ganso, reassuring in his familiarity at Santos. Even though this was still a young team, there was plenty of experience.

Dani Alves from Barcelona, Thiago Silva and

Alexandre Pato from A.C. Milan, as well as Chelsea's Ramires and Liverpool's Lucas Leiva helped make up a formidable side.

In the opening minutes, Neymar had a few early touches, but was mostly kept quiet by the USA defence.

But the new-look Brazil team started to settle into their rhythm and, after 29 minutes, a searching pass from Ramires set the left-back, André Santos, off down the left wing.

Santos glanced up, before swinging in a perfect first-time cross. Neymar ran towards the back post, meeting the ball cleanly with a firm header. It sailed into the bottom corner, with the USA keeper, Tim Howard, planted to the spot.

GOAL!

Neymar sank to his knees, too overwhelmed to say anything. He'd scored for Brazil – and on his debut too.

This was the sort of thing he'd dreamed of as a young boy and now, here he was, living it.

Ganso was the first to congratulate him. "What's with all these headers, Ney?" he asked with a grin. "I thought you were supposed to be a flair player!"

"I wouldn't have cared if that had bounced in off my knee!" Neymar replied, his face beaming.

Just before half-time, Ganso carried the ball forward and passed to Ramires, who played a through ball to the Brazil forwards.

Moments later it was 2-0.

Now, as a contest, the game was already over. Brazil had settled in – and they were cruising.

In the second half, with the pressure off, Brazil could enjoy themselves.

Shortly after the restart, a shot from Neymar was blocked, and Pato fired the rebound against the post.

"I'd have scored that one, no doubt!" Neymar called. Pato just chuckled and shook his head.

Minutes later, Neymar picked up a sweeping cross-field pass from Dani Alves. He did two step-overs to wrong-foot the USA defender, then drilled a shot on goal, which the keeper barely managed to palm away.

Neymar turned to see Pato grinning at him.

"Maybe you still have a few things to learn from me, with finishing like that!" Pato called out, putting his arm around Neymar's shoulder.

Neymar had one more sight of goal, running onto a through ball from Dani Alves and getting a shot away, but, again, it was saved by the substitute keeper, Brad Guzan.

Shortly afterwards, Neymar was subbed off. He applauded the crowd as he walked off the pitch, and the Brazil fans responded with a standing ovation.

He'd taken two more huge steps in his career – his first international appearance, and his first goal for Brazil.

Here he was, playing with the best players from his country, and it felt as if he was having a kick-about with his friends.

If there'd been any lingering nerves or doubts – after this game, they'd vanished.

9
THE NEW PRINCE

June 2011, Estádio do Pacaembu, São Paulo, Brazil
Copa Libertadores Final 2nd Leg, Santos v Peñarol

"Santos haven't won the Libertadores since 1963, when Pelé and Zito were playing," the Santos manager, Muricy Ramalho, began, looking at the Santos players who were gathered around him in the dressing room. "So, today you aren't just playing the opposition – you're playing against nearly fifty years of history," he continued.

"Those players are in the stadium watching today, so make sure you go out there and show them who the new Santos heroes are!" he declared boldly.

The players all cheered and jumped to their feet, eager to get out onto the pitch.

Muricy pulled Neymar aside and quietly whispered in his ear. "Pelé won it for us in the 1960s. We had the star of Brazilian football then. Today, it's your turn to shine – as Santos' new star."

Neymar nodded with quiet confidence. He'd continued to improve over the past year, and had led Santos to win the Paulista state league. He'd also been Santos' main inspiration on their run to the final of the Copa Libertadores, the South American club championship.

As the players walked out onto the pitch, Neymar was surprised by the intensity of the crowd. Flares were lit around the stadium, and tens of thousands of fans were in full voice, as smoke drifted across the pitch.

"This is it, Ney," Ganso shouted, over the noise of the crowd. "One more game to become champions of South America. And it sounds like these fans want it just as much as we do!"

Santos had drawn the first leg of the final, against the Uruguayan champions, Peñarol, 0-0. Today, they had the chance to win the Libertadores in the return leg in Brazil.

"We need to win this one. You heard the boss – we'll be heroes forever if we do," Neymar shouted to Ganso.

The early stages of the game were cagey and physical. Repeatedly, Neymar was fouled by the tough-tackling Uruguayan players, desperate to stop him threatening their goal. He was getting frustrated.

"Don't worry, Ney. You're panicking them already," Elano called out, trying to reassure his team-mate.

Half an hour later, the ball broke loose on the halfway line. Neymar and a Peñarol player spotted it at the same time, and both players raced towards it.

Neymar refused to pull out of the challenge, determined not to be intimidated by the Uruguayan players, but he went for the ball with his studs raised and planted his foot on the opposition player's shin.

He was shown a yellow card by the referee. One more mistake and he would be out of the biggest game of his life.

At half-time it was still 0-0. So far, Peñarol had managed to keep Neymar out of the game.

In the dressing room, Elano pulled Neymar and Ganso aside. As the senior player in the squad, having already played in Europe for Man City, his younger team-mates always listened when he had something to say.

"Don't get too frustrated," Elano began. "We still have 45 minutes to play. They'll get tired chasing your shadows soon, I know it. If you're patient, one bit of magic, or one combination from you two, will be enough to win the game."

Then he turned to Neymar and grinned. "Oh, and Ney – don't try any more tackles. Leave that to the defenders!"

Elano was right. Two minutes after the restart, Ganso received the ball in the middle of the pitch and, without looking, flicked it behind him into the path of Arouca. Arouca dribbled past two players, before laying the ball off to Neymar on the edge of the area.

First time, Neymar fizzed the ball into the near corner of the goal, surprising the keeper, who was expecting him to open his body for a shot into the far corner.

"YESS!!" Neymar cried, running towards the corner flag. The noise from the Santos fans filled the stadium, as Neymar was swamped by his celebrating team-mates.

After he finally escaped their embraces, he turned alone to the crowd, and sucked his thumb. Many of the fans knew exactly what Neymar was signalling – he was going to be a father, with a son due to be born in two months' time.

This was Neymar's idea of a perfect present. His son would be able to look back at this moment, in the biggest game of his father's career so far, and see a goal dedicated to him.

"Make sure you stay focused," Elano shouted across to Neymar. "Don't let that celebration be wasted – nobody wants to remember a goal in a game they went on to lose."

"Don't worry, I've got this!" Neymar answered. "You're welcome to chip in with a goal, if you can!" he added with a grin.

Twenty minutes later, with Santos still 1-0 up, Neymar received the ball on the left wing. He paused, standing completely still and looking for options.

Spotting the movement of Elano in the middle, he laid the ball off to him. Elano then found the Santos right-back, Danilo, sprinting down the right wing.

Danilo ran forward, reaching the penalty area, before checking onto his left foot and curling the ball into the bottom corner.

Goal! Santos were now 2-0 up – and comfortable.

"How's that for chipping in?" called Elano, as they all celebrated.

Ten minutes later, Peñarol pulled one back, with a lucky own-goal which looped in off an unsuspecting Santos defender.

Santos had ten minutes left to hold out.

"The best form of defence is attack!" Neymar shouted to the Santos players around him. He knew that playing too negatively would invite pressure.

He kept charging at the Peñarol defence, trying for a third goal which would seal the win.

With only a few minutes left, Neymar ran onto a through ball from Elano, passing the tiring defenders. As the keeper came rushing out, Neymar clipped the ball over him, then agonisingly watched it roll against the post. Zé Eduardo followed up for Santos, but he could only fire the ball against the post again, sending it out of play.

Moments later, the miss was forgiven, as the referee blew the final whistle. Santos – and Neymar – had done it. They had won the Libertadores.

As the players danced together in the centre circle, they were joined by former Santos players, including Zito.

"I knew you'd be able to do this, when I watched you all those years ago!" he said breathlessly, hugging Neymar tightly. "And now, there's someone I'd like you to meet."

Neymar turned to see Pelé walking towards him, grinning broadly.

"So, you're the new Prince of Santos!" he said, embracing Neymar.

Neymar couldn't believe it. He'd won the Libertadores, and now he was being embraced by the best football player of all time.

"That was amazing," Pelé whispered in his ear. "You keep this up, you'll become a true legend of football!"

10
SPAIN, PART TWO

June 2013, Camp Nou, Barcelona, Spain

As Neymar walked out onto the pitch at the Camp Nou for the first time, he was met by the cheers of thousands of fans.

"Neymar, Neymar!" The sound rang around the stadium.

But this wasn't for a match. This was for his presentation – as the newest signing to FC Barcelona.

He'd taken the eleven-hour flight from São Paulo on a private jet and, on landing, had been swamped by the media at the airport.

He was exhausted and jet-lagged, just running on adrenaline. But despite all of that, he felt as if he was finally growing up – moving to Europe to fulfil his dream of playing for a top European club.

Outside the stadium, he had seemingly endless photos taken, with hundreds of photographers jostling to get the best shot. He'd then undertaken a series of medicals, before being whisked off to sign contracts, ahead of his grand unveiling.

His father had been with him throughout. They hadn't really had much chance to talk to each other since their plane landed, but Neymar Senior was a reassuring presence every step of the way.

As Neymar walked out onto the pitch, wearing a crisp new Barcelona kit, he felt a little awkward. What was he supposed to do now?

Then someone rolled him a ball. Finally – this was something that made him feel comfortable.

He flicked the ball up and down, back and forth, from

foot to foot, as the fans showed their appreciation. Then he started putting on a show, breaking out more and more extravagant tricks, executing each one with ease. Every one of the fans in the stadium could suddenly see the quality of their new signing.

Then, finally, Neymar was interviewed on the pitch for the watching crowd.

"First question, Neymar. Why was now the time to move to Europe?" the interviewer asked.

Neymar thought about his conversations with the Brazil manager, Mano Menezes, a few months ago. Neymar had just scored a hat-trick in an 8-0 win for Brazil, against China.

"This is getting too easy for you now, isn't it?" Menezes had asked, as they'd walked back to the dressing room after the match.

"I would have scored even more if you hadn't taken me off!" Neymar had answered with a smile.

"It's the same for you at Santos now too. You've been the star there for four years. It's time to make the next step up," Menezes had said, a serious look on his face.

"The plan was always to wait until after the 2014

World Cup," Neymar had answered. "That's when my contract with Santos ends."

"Too late. To be the best at the World Cup, you need to test yourself. Europe is the only way to do that," Menezes had urged. "Santos are struggling. They haven't even qualified for the next Libertadores. You need a stage to perform on, Neymar."

Now, standing on the pitch at Camp Nou, Neymar could look back and see that what the Brazil manager had been saying was right. Santos had become his comfort zone, and he needed to make the next step up.

He was sure now that leaving his childhood club had been the right thing to do.

"Barcelona is the best place to continue my development," Neymar replied to the interviewer. "This is the best club to help me become the best player I can be."

"And win a few trophies for us here too, of course!" the interviewer added. "OK – next question. How do you feel, knowing that Barcelona paid 57 million euros for you? Does that kind of money bring any pressure?"

"I don't worry about the numbers," Neymar smiled.

"My father deals with all the business stuff. I just know that – well, the money is OK, but it really doesn't buy happiness."

He paused, then continued. "I had a lot of offers from different clubs – Chelsea, Real Madrid … but I followed my heart – to Barcelona."

"Final question," the interviewer said. "How does it feel to be joining a team like Barcelona? You're joining a team that includes Lionel Messi, who's won his fourth consecutive Ballon d'Or for the best player in the world."

"The best is here – and that's Messi. I'm one of the luckiest players in the world to be able to play with him – and it's an honour," Neymar answered.

He paused and moved a little closer to the microphone. "Here, I have the opportunity to play with great players I admire – like Messi, Xavi and Andrés Iniesta. I've begun a new stage in my life. I know I'm going to be very happy here, and I know I'm going to achieve great things with this great club."

II
GOLDEN

June 2013, Maracanã, Rio de Janeiro, Brazil
Confederations Cup Final, Brazil v Spain

Neymar looked across at the Spain players standing next to him in the tunnel, waiting to head out onto the pitch.

He could see players that he'd soon be playing with at Barcelona – Xavi, Andrés Iniesta, Sergio Busquets and Gerard Piqué.

"Come on, Ney. Focus!" Fred called over. "The best way to make a good first impression is to let your feet do the talking!" As Brazil's veteran centre-forward, Fred had the respect of the rest of the players. They always listened to him.

So far in the tournament, Neymar had scored in each of the group games, ensuring that Brazil sailed through to the final.

Their opponents in the final were reigning World Cup winners Spain – a side that hadn't lost for over three years. Twenty-nine games unbeaten.

As the players filed out onto the pitch, the Brazil fans in the famous Maracanã stadium rose to greet them, blowing horns and cheering loudly.

This Confederations Cup was a warm-up event for the World Cup that was due to be held in Brazil the following year. Neymar was very aware how much it would mean to the Brazil fans if they were able to lift the trophy at home.

Just two minutes into the game, the Brazil fans got exactly what they were hoping for. Hulk swung in a deep cross from the right wing, which sailed towards Neymar at the back post. He couldn't anticipate the flight of the ball, which bounced awkwardly off his shin, but it fell kindly for Fred, who hooked the ball over the keeper, into the back of the net.

The Brazil players ran to the corner flag together to celebrate, as the stadium erupted.

"Some assist that was!" Fred laughed. "All you have to do is stand there and you make things happen!"

"I'm just trying to make you look good – it's hard work!" Neymar replied, with a broad grin.

The remainder of the first half wasn't quite so smooth. Spain showed their class by fighting their way back into the game, pressuring Brazil hard.

About twenty minutes in, Juan Mata played a one-two and broke through the Brazil backline, then squared the ball perfectly to Pedro. He shaped his body and curled the ball past Júlio Cesar in the Brazil goal. Neymar held his breath but, just before the ball rippled the net, David Luiz miraculously reached out and deflected the ball over the bar.

The Brazil fans, as well as the players, all let out a huge sigh of relief.

Neymar wasn't going to ignore that wake-up call.

A minute before half-time, he picked up the ball

near the Spain penalty area, with numerous defenders around him. He only had one thought on his mind, so, taking a touch to set himself, he rocketed a shot past Iker Casillas in the Spain goal.

Now Brazil were 2-0 up – against infallible Spain.

Without hesitating, Neymar ran towards the Brazil fans, his arms outstretched as he celebrated the goal with them. As he reached the fans, he was immediately swamped by his team-mates. If this was what it was like for the Confederations Cup, he couldn't wait for the World Cup.

Luiz Felipe Scolari, the new Brazil manager, only had a few words at half-time. "Brazil have struggled in the last few years, in the Copa América and in the Olympics," he said. "The fans will forget all that, if you win here in front of them. Let all of Brazil see what you can do, and then let them get excited about the World Cup!"

Two minutes after the restart, Brazil got a third.

Hulk used his strength to hold off a defender in the middle of the pitch, before laying the ball into the path of Neymar.

He ran over the ball, distracting the defenders who assumed he would take it in his stride. Instead, it rolled through to unmarked Fred, who swept the ball into the net.

"See, I don't even need to touch the ball to assist you now!" Neymar called.

"I'm pretty sure you're a goal behind me now for the Golden Boot, Ney. Try to keep up!" Fred laughed.

Spain weren't finished, however, and soon won a penalty, when Marcelo clipped Jesús Navas in the box.

Sergio Ramos stepped up but, obviously feeling the pressure, dragged his penalty wide.

The game finished 3-0, with Brazil adding another trophy to their cabinet.

Then, after the presentation, Neymar was awarded the Golden Ball, for best player at the tournament.

He was delighted. He had won his first trophy with Brazil, and had played a critical role in every game.

And even better, Brazil had beaten Spain, of all teams – ending their unbeaten record.

Neymar had shown his future Barcelona team-mates (and opponents!) how good he could be.

He'd also reminded the Brazil fans what they could expect in the World Cup next summer – especially as, by then, he would have had a season of top-level European football under his belt.

He couldn't wait for it.

12
SIX MINUTES

July 2014, Santos, São Paulo, Brazil

With only moments to go before Brazil's World Cup semi-final against Germany, the roars of the crowd filled the Mineirão stadium, home of Brazilian football.

Neymar was in Brazil too – but he was sitting in his parents' home, watching the game on television.

This hadn't been the plan.

His first season with Barcelona hadn't been easy.

They'd finished runners-up in both La Liga and the Copa del Rey – and they'd been knocked out of the Champions League in the quarter-finals.

It had taken Neymar most of the season to adapt to the faster, more physical style of Spanish football – but he had regained his form in time for the World Cup.

The tournament had started well for him. Brazil had breezed through the group stage, and he'd scored four goals in the three games.

In the first knockout round, Brazil had edged out Chile on penalties, with Neymar scoring the winning spot-kick.

Then came the quarter-final against Colombia. Just seven minutes in, Neymar had swung in a deep corner, which Thiago Silva had bundled over the line to give Brazil the lead.

Then, with an hour gone, Brazil had won a free kick, 30 yards from goal. David Luiz had stepped up and fired the ball into the top corner. Brazil were on their way.

Colombia had scored a late consolation, when Júlio César conceded a penalty for a foul on Carlos Bacca, which James Rodríguez had calmly tucked away.

But the biggest drama was still to come.

With just five minutes left to play, Brazil had scrambled to defend a Colombia corner. The Brazil defence had cleared the ball as far as Neymar, and as he'd tried to control it, he'd felt a shooting pain through his spine. The Colombia defender, Juan Camilo Zúñiga, had jumped for the ball, and his knee had connected with Neymar's back.

Neymar had lain on the floor in pain, and Marcelo had frantically rushed over to him.

"Get the doctors!" he'd called out to the bench.

"No, no, I want to keep playing," Neymar had said weakly. He'd been desperate to score. This was the World Cup – he could play through it.

Neymar had tried to get up, but couldn't. He couldn't lift his legs, he couldn't *feel* his legs. He'd cried as the doctors had lifted him onto a stretcher and carried him off the pitch.

Neymar had known it had to be serious when he'd realised that the team doctors were sending him straight to hospital.

There, he'd undergone a series of scans on his back.

"I have good news and bad news," the doctor had told him, examining one of Neymar's scans.

"Give me the bad news first."

"Your World Cup is over. Even if Brazil get to the final, you won't be able to play. You've broken a vertebra in your back."

"What's the good news?" Neymar had asked, wondering what could possibly soften the blow of missing out on playing for Brazil – in Brazil – in a World Cup final.

"The good news is that you're very lucky. You *will* be able to play football again. If it had been just two centimetres closer to your spine, your football career would be over."

Neymar had spent the following week at home with his parents, in São Paulo. His mum had cried when she'd first seen him wearing his spinal brace, and he'd cried with her. After all the time he'd spent dreaming about this World Cup, now he couldn't even see it through.

But then, later in the week, Neymar had received a note from Pelé.

"Neymar, I was also injured during the 1962 World

Cup in Chile, and I was out for the rest of the tournament. God helped Brazil continue on to win the tournament. I'm sure the same will happen with the team in this World Cup, and you will still be a world champion."

Pelé had been right – Neymar could still win this World Cup. He knew his team-mates were good enough to win, even without him.

Besides, he'd already contributed so much in helping them get as far as the semi-finals. Nobody could doubt his impact.

Pelé's note had helped to lift Neymar's spirits, and he'd begun to look forward to the semi-final.

The family gathered around the television for the match – his mother and his father sitting either side of him.

Neymar thought about how far his family had come, since living in the cramped apartment in São Vicente, all those years ago. That felt like a lifetime ago now.

Most pundits agreed that Brazil and Germany were the two strongest teams in the tournament, and that the winner of this semi-final would likely go on to win the final – and be World Cup champions.

As the players lined up for the national anthems, Neymar Senior suddenly pointed at the television.

"It's your shirt, Júnior!" he called out excitedly.

Sure enough, Júlio César and David Luiz were holding up a shirt between them, as they belted out the Brazilian anthem. Now Neymar could see it – his shirt. Neymar Jr – 10. He was there with them in spirit. Together, they could do this.

As the game got underway, Brazil had the first chance after just three minutes, with Marcelo shooting wide. Neymar jumped up as the shot flashed past the post.

"Sit down, Júnior!" his mother called. "You need to stay still and rest."

"There's no way I'll be sitting still if we win!" Neymar replied quickly.

But then, in the 11th minute, everything changed. Toni Kroos whipped in a corner for Germany, and Thomas Müller broke free of his marker, before guiding the ball into the net. It was 1-0 to Germany.

Then, in the 23rd minute, Müller and Kroos combined to set up Miroslav Klose. He tucked away the rebound, after Júlio César had saved his first effort. 2-0 to Germany.

In the 24th minute, Philipp Lahm's deflected cross fell to Kroos, who hammered a low shot into the Brazil goal. 3-0.

In the 26th minute, Kroos stole the ball on the halfway line, played a one-two with Sami Khedira and rolled the ball past the keeper into the net. 4-0.

In the 29th minute, Khedira broke forward, exchanged passes with Mesut Özil and fired in a goal himself.

It was 5-0 to Germany.

In the space of just six minutes, Germany had totally destroyed Brazil.

The camera in the stadium panned to the crowd, showing the Brazil fans shocked and in tears.

The Neymar household couldn't process what they'd just seen. Neymar turned in stunned silence to his mother, who had tears in her eyes, and then to his father, who was shaking his head in disbelief.

This was supposed to be Brazil's great moment – and instead they were being humiliated in their own back yard. Brazil had won more World Cups than any other nation. They were the masters of the beautiful game, and had produced more thrilling players than any other country. Yet here they were, being taught a serious lesson, on the biggest stage of all.

By half-time, most of the Brazil fans had already left the stadium, but Neymar had nowhere to go. He remained planted on the sofa, scarcely believing what had just happened.

He wondered what he'd be telling his team-mates in the dressing room at half-time, if he was there. But, then again, if he'd been playing, then perhaps it wouldn't have turned out like this.

The second half didn't get much better.

In the 69th minute, Lahm fizzed a low cross into the path of André Schürrle, who stroked the ball past the keeper from six yards out. 6-0 to Germany.

Then, in the 79th minute, Schürrle ran onto Müller's cross, before thumping the ball off the crossbar and into César's goal. 7-0.

It was then that those Brazil fans who had remained in the stadium all stood up and began to applaud the German players.

As football fans, they had witnessed a complete performance. And, even though it had ended their dream of a Brazil World Cup victory, they couldn't help but appreciate the brilliant football they had seen.

Back in the Neymar household, Neymar felt the nagging pain in his back as he rose gingerly to his feet and turned off the television.

"I don't want to watch this," he said.

13
CHAMPIONS

June 2015, Olympiastadion, Berlin, Germany
Champions League Final, Barcelona v Juventus

"This one's for Xavi," Andrés Iniesta reminded his team-mates. "One last game for us to give him the perfect send-off."

The Barcelona players began the familiar march down the tunnel and out onto the pitch – this time, for the biggest game in club football. The Champions League final.

Barca had already won La Liga and the Copa del Rey, both during Neymar's successful second season with the club. Now, they had the chance to win the treble.

This was to be Xavi's final game for Barcelona, after representing the club for 767 games in 17 years. The Barca players were determined to make it a game they'd all remember.

After he'd returned from injury in the autumn, Neymar had channelled his World Cup frustrations onto the pitch.

He'd been Barca's top scorer in the Copa del Rey, and was behind only Messi and Ronaldo for goals in La Liga. His role in Barcelona winning both competitions had been crucial.

He'd also been inspirational in the Champions League, and was now only one goal behind Messi and Ronaldo (again) for top scorer. But now he was about to play in the biggest game of his life.

"How many goals are you getting today, Leo?" Neymar asked, grinning at Messi as they walked out of the tunnel.

"I've already got 58 this season. So I might go easy today, just so you can catch up!" Messi smiled.

Between them, Messi, Luis Suárez, and Neymar had scored 120 goals over the course of the season. The trio had been dubbed "MSN" for short, and had become the most-feared attacking trio in world football.

As the last notes of the Champions League anthem echoed around the Olympiastadion, Neymar looked across at the Juventus players. He wondered whether they were afraid of facing Barcelona today.

They should be, he thought.

Just four minutes into the game, Jordi Alba received a long ball on the left wing, then passed it straight to Neymar. He slowly dribbled forward with the ball, drawing three Juventus defenders towards him, then released it for Iniesta, who burst into the space Neymar had created.

Iniesta pulled the ball back, and Ivan Rakitić deftly swept it into the Juventus goal.

"GOAL!" shouted the Barca fans, as the Barcelona players gathered around the corner flag in celebration. It was the perfect start.

The rest of the first half was comparatively uneventful. Both sides knew what was at stake, and neither team wanted to risk losing the game by sending too many players forward in attack.

Juventus had come into the game in search of their own treble, having won the Serie A and the Coppa Italia, and they were good enough – and determined enough – to stop Barca from running away with it.

Early in the second half, Carlos Tevez fired a speculative shot from the edge of the area, which Barca keeper Marc-André ter Stegen could only parry. Álvaro Morata was first to the ball, and made no mistake from close range.

Juventus had levelled.

Despite the goal, Barca's confidence wasn't shaken, and slowly the momentum in the game swung back in their direction.

After 68 minutes, Messi burst forward, brushing off a Juventus defender as if he wasn't there. Messi fizzed a shot at goal, but it was pushed away by Gianluigi Buffon. In a carbon copy of Juventus' equaliser, Suárez was first to the ball, lifting it into the goal.

Barcelona were back in control.

Two minutes later, Alba swung a perfect cross in from the left, and Neymar jumped above the two defenders to head the ball past the keeper and into the goal.

"Yes!" he shouted cautiously. Had the ball flicked off his hand as he'd headed it? He wasn't sure.

But the referee was sure. He'd spotted the ball hitting Neymar's hand, and he chalked the goal off for handball. It was still 2-1.

In the 78th minute, Iniesta was subbed off, and was replaced by Xavi – for his final ever Barcelona appearance.

Even at 35 years of age, Xavi was still a top player. Now he started to control the flow of the game, moving the ball about with ease.

As the minutes ticked away, Neymar felt conflicting emotions. He was about to win the biggest trophy of his career, completing a treble-winning season. But he hadn't scored in this game. He hadn't left his mark.

Then, in the 96th minute, Juventus won a corner – and the whole stadium held its breath.

The corner was poor. The Barca defence cleared the

ball to the edge of the area, and then suddenly hooked it to the halfway line.

Neymar was the only Barcelona player there to receive it. He carried the ball forward to the edge of the Juventus area, before playing a quick one-two with Pedro, who'd sprinted to catch up with him.

Neymar took a touch, before firing the ball under Buffon, into the net.

3-1 to Barcelona – now it was game over.

Neymar ran to the fans, pulling his shirt over his head in celebration. He could feel all the frustrations of the last year just melting away.

He was back.

14
REDEMPTION

August 2016, Maracanã, Rio de Janeiro, Brazil
Olympic Football Final, Brazil v Germany

"Are you worrying about the game, Júnior?" Neymar Senior asked, sounding concerned.

They were sitting in the team hotel, early on Saturday morning, on the day of the Olympic football final.

Neymar Senior knew that his son had been struggling with the pressure – not just of being the star player, but also being the captain of the squad. And this year, the Olympics were being held at home, in Brazil.

"The fans were outside the stadium for the whole of last night, singing and cheering. Don't they realise we need our sleep?" Neymar answered wearily.

"People in Brazil need this," his father replied. "Winning the Olympics would be a real consolation for the pain of losing the World Cup so badly. This is the only trophy we've never won. Just think – winning it here, at the Maracanã, and beating Germany to win it. That would be sweet!"

"That doesn't help, Dad!" complained Neymar.

"You know your mother and I are so proud of you, regardless of what happens today. You've carried the hopes of the country on your shoulders. That's pretty amazing, for a boy from Mogi das Cruzes."

"I might ask the manager if I can give up the captaincy after today," Neymar confided, changing the subject. "What do you think?"

Neymar Senior looked at his son thoughtfully. "It's up to you, Júnior. Nobody will mind if you want to share out some of the responsibility. But look, you don't make any decisions now," he added. "Let's just focus on today's game. Tell me again who's starting … "

Germany kicked off, as the noise of the crowd reached fever-pitch. Everybody was well aware that there was more at stake in this game than just the Olympic final.

Ten minutes in, Germany had the first chance. Their winger, Serge Gnabry, beat his man on the left wing and laid the ball into the path of Julian Brandt, who opened his body up and curled the ball against the Brazil crossbar.

After this wake-up call, Neymar went on a jinking run at the German defence. He dodged multiple tackles, before being clattered on the edge of the area by Matthias Ginter.

There was no doubt who would take the free-kick. Neymar stood over the ball, 25 yards out, and took a deep breath. Then he ran up, fired a shot towards the top corner and watched the ball crash off the crossbar into the net. 1-0 to Brazil.

"YESSS!" he roared, as he sprinted towards the Brazil bench in celebration.

Shortly after the restart, Julian Brandt crossed in a free kick from the right wing, which was met by Sven Bender. His header slammed into the bar and flew out of play for a goal kick.

The Brazil goal was living a charmed life, and Neymar began to hope that today might be their day after all.

Germany were far from finished, though. Just minutes into the second-half, their right-back, Jeremy Toljan, floated a dangerous cross into the Brazil penalty area. The Germany striker, Max Meyer, rushed onto the ball and swept it clinically past Weverton in the Brazil goal.

Germany were level.

"Come on, guys! Focus! We can do this!" Neymar called to his team-mates. He wasn't going to let the disaster of the World Cup repeat itself.

Despite his best efforts, there were no more goals, and the 90 minutes came to an end with the scores level.

After 30 minutes of extra time, the scores were unchanged. The teams would need to be separated by a penalty shootout.

The Brazil players stood around as their manager,

Rogério Micale, read out the list of penalty takers. Neymar was fifth – he would be taking the last of Brazil's penalties, before it went to sudden death.

Germany went first. Ginter stepped up and comfortably fired his penalty into the bottom corner. 1-0 Germany.

Renato Augusto stepped up first for Brazil. He kept his nerve, smashing his penalty high into the top corner. 1-1.

Next, Gnabry came forward for Germany, looking nervous. His penalty was weak, but it managed to sneak past Weverton in the Brazil goal. 2-1 Germany.

The PSG defender, Marquinhos, stepped up next for Brazil. He calmly sent the keeper the wrong way. 2-2.

Neymar watched from the halfway line, one arm around each of the team-mates either side of him. Nobody said a word. Everybody was focused on their own role, nervously counting down the shots until it was their turn – although they all hoped they wouldn't be needed.

Except for Neymar. He was desperate for his chance to score.

Julian Brandt was up next for Germany. It was his turn to send the keeper the wrong way. 3-2.

Rafinha went next for Brazil. He was ice-cool, disguising his run-up and rolling his penalty along the ground. 3-3.

Niklas Süle, the big German defender, strode up and punted his penalty as hard as he could, somehow finding the bottom corner. 4-3.

Luan was fourth to go for Brazil. He didn't even look up from the ball once, as he confidently swept it in. 4-4.

Next, Nils Petersen, for Germany, took a long run up, before miskicking his penalty. Weverton stood strong, and comfortably saved it. Now it was 4-4 – with Brazil holding the advantage.

The Brazil players in the centre circle started jumping and celebrating – all except for Neymar, who began to take the long walk towards the penalty spot.

It had all come down to this one kick. If he scored, Brazil would win Olympic Gold.

Neymar picked the ball up, found the valve, and placed the ball on the spot in his usual position.

The tension in the stadium was unbearable. Many of

the Brazil fans were hiding behind their hands, unable to watch.

Showing no emotion, Neymar took a long run-up and, as he reached the ball, he stuttered – once, then twice. The keeper moved to his right, and then Neymar opened his body up and despatched the ball into the top-left corner. No goalkeeper could have saved it, even if they knew where it was going.

Brazil had won Olympic Gold – and Neymar had scored the winning goal.

Neymar started to jog calmly towards the screaming fans but, moments later, his composure evaporated and he joined his team-mates in wild celebrations.

He fell to his knees, raised his hands to the sky and started to sob.

He cried for the pressure he'd been under as captain, carrying the dreams of a nation at just 24 years of age.

He cried for the national shame of being thrashed by Germany in the Mineirão, and for the relief of finally being able to avenge the loss.

And he cried for becoming the only player who had ever led Brazil to an Olympic football gold medal.

15
TO MOVE OR NOT TO MOVE

August 2017, Barcelona, Spain

"It would be a world-record transfer, Júnior," Neymar Senior told his son. "Two hundred and twenty two million euros is more than double the current record transfer fee."

He paused, then added, "But I'm not sure it's the right move for you. Barcelona have been good for you – and good *to* you. You've won everything here."

"Not everything," replied Neymar, sharply.

They were sitting in a hotel room in Barcelona. The Paris Saint-Germain director of football was downstairs, in a meeting with the club's lawyers. They were waiting for Neymar's decision. Would he or wouldn't he join PSG? He still hadn't decided.

"Can I become the best player in the world at Barca?" Neymar said slowly, asking himself as much as his father. "I can win club trophies for sure, but I've already won them all," he added.

He was torn. Every decision up to this point in his career had felt easy. There'd always seemed to be a clear correct answer.

This was why, now, he was grateful to be able to talk it over with his father. In recent years, his dad had become his key adviser in developing his career – and Neymar had found it invaluable.

"Messi will always be the star at Barcelona," his dad offered. "He's the hero who came from their academy. But you can still become what you want to be, here at Barca. You can make a difference by winning with Brazil."

"Is the French league good enough? Is there a challenge there?" Neymar asked.

"Maybe not as good as Spain. But moving would mean that you could focus more on the Champions League – and on Brazil," replied Neymar Senior.

Neymar thought back to his last training session with Barcelona. The newspapers had been full of reports that he might move, but during that training session nobody had mentioned anything to him.

Then, afterwards, as he'd got changed, Messi and Suárez had approached him, together.

"Ney, if you want to win everything, stay here with us," Suárez had urged.

"Haven't we already won everything?" Neymar had replied. He hadn't wanted to tell them that he was now thinking about personal achievements, rather than team trophies.

"If you have to move, move to England. The football is better – it's more suited to you. Maybe Manchester City. But France … " Suárez had left the rest unsaid.

Neymar had felt obliged to justify the move to his team-mates, even though he'd still been unsure.

"The project there is amazing," he'd told them. "And the players too – Edinson Cavani, and guys I know from Brazil – Thiago Silva, Marquinhos, Lucas Moura. Even Dani Alves has just signed. They can't all be wrong!"

"You're different from those players, Ney, and you know it," Messi had replied, speaking for the first time. "You can win the Ballon d'Or. They can't."

Neymar had looked up sharply. Messi, of all people, should understand why Neymar might want to leave. He and Cristiano Ronaldo had won every Ballon d'Or for a decade, ever since Kaká in 2007.

Deep down, Neymar knew that the very fact that Messi was so comfortably the best player in world, was exactly the reason why he wanted to leave Barca.

"If you stay at Barcelona, you'll win the Ballon d'Or, for sure. And I can help you," Messi had told him.

Neymar had never doubted Messi's intentions, but he could tell that Messi hadn't appreciated the position Neymar had been in.

Neymar had known that, while Messi was at Barcelona, Neymar would never be able to surpass him.

To be recognised as the best in the world, Neymar

needed to forge his own path, stepping outside of Messi's shadow.

Back in the hotel room, Neymar looked across at his father.

"Will you come to Paris with me? Will Mum and Rafaella visit?"

"Of course, Júnior. You know we'll support you, whatever decision you make. But you will have to decide at some point – those men downstairs won't wait forever," Neymar Senior answered warmly.

"OK – I'm ready. I'm moving to PSG."

Neymar followed his father downstairs, ready to agree to the biggest football transfer of all time.

16
DÉJÀ VU

July 2018, Kazan Arena, Kazan, Russia
World Cup Quarter-Final, Brazil, v Belgium

"How's the injury feeling, Ney?" asked Thiago Silva.

Neymar was sitting in the dressing room, strapping his foot up, before pulling on his boot.

"It feels like every time there's a World Cup, people start asking me that question!" Neymar replied, trying to hide his frustration from his team-mates.

His first season at Paris Saint-Germain had been

going exactly as he'd hoped. He'd scored 28 goals in his first 30 games, and PSG had been on track to compete for every available trophy.

But then, in February, he'd faced Marseille in Le Classique – the biggest derby in French football.

The match itself had gone well, with PSG walking away with a 3-0 win. But in the 76th minute, Neymar's foot had been clipped by a defender and, as he'd landed, it had twisted painfully.

He'd felt a sudden jolt, and had known it must have been bad. He'd been stretchered off the pitch, and had been on crutches until the swelling had gone down enough for a doctor to examine it.

"You've broken your foot," the doctor had said. "It will need an operation. You'll be out of action for months – the World Cup will be touch and go."

Neymar's heart had sunk at hearing this news, which had felt painfully familiar. But at least with this injury, he'd had time to rest and to recover.

He hadn't played for PSG for the rest of the season, as they'd gone on to win the domestic treble – Ligue 1, the Coupe de France, and the Coupe de la Ligue.

Neymar hadn't really taken part in the celebrations. He hadn't played for the last three months, and had spent that time worrying about getting fit for Russia, where the World Cup was being hosted.

"Well, it's held up pretty well, so far," replied Thiago Silva, enthusiastically. "Now it just has to last three more games!"

"That's only if we get to the final!" Marcelo interjected. "Don't get ahead of yourself – Belgium are pretty good."

Neymar had recovered just in time for the World Cup, with his first appearance being in Brazil's warm-up friendly – their last game before the tournament.

He'd played every minute of the tournament so far and, although his foot had held up, he was tired.

"Let's just get through the next 90 minutes first!" he called out, keen to change the subject.

As the teams lined up, he looked across at the Belgium players. Marcelo was right – their team was full of quality players.

Kevin De Bruyne, Eden Hazard and Romelu Lukaku were all in the starting line-up. This was Belgium's golden generation – they would be a serious test for Brazil.

The game started well for Brazil, with the players going on the attack in the first ten minutes.

Neymar created the opening chance of the game. He swung in a dangerous corner from the left, which Thiago Silva could only manage to divert onto the post, narrowly missing the target.

Then, three minutes later, Belgium whipped in a corner of their own. It was directed at Vincent Kompany, their big centre-back. He missed the ball, but it flicked off the shoulder of Fernandinho and bounced agonisingly into the Brazil net, for an own goal.

Belgium had the lead. Now they were in the ascendancy.

"Heads up, boys!" called Neymar, trying to rally the troops.

Shortly afterwards, Romelu Lukaku received the ball deep in his own half and drove forwards. Using his immense strength, he shrugged off one, then two, defenders, drawing closer to Brazil's goal.

He then laid the ball off to Kevin De Bruyne, on the

edge of the Brazil penalty area. Without even looking up, De Bruyne fired an unstoppable drive past the Brazil keeper, Alisson.

2-0 to Belgium.

Now Brazil were in real trouble. Neymar thought they'd exorcised the demons from the 2014 loss to Germany, but he could sense the fear creeping back in.

Brazil responded well in the rest of the half, creating a number of chances and testing the Belgium keeper, Thibaut Courtois, at every opportunity. But they weren't able to score.

At half-time, Brazil trudged off glumly.

"I told you we needed to worry about this game – not get distracted by semi-finals and finals. We need to win this game – and we can," Neymar told his team-mates, trying to rally them. "Some of us might not be playing in the next tournament. I know how close I was to not playing here at all. So don't let this chance slip by."

Brazil had 45 minutes left to overturn a two-goal deficit – or Neymar's World Cup would end at the quarter-final stage, yet again.

When Brazil came back out for the second-half,

Neymar's pep-talk seemed to have worked. The players were sharper, working harder and closing down more quickly.

Brazil had two early claims for a penalty, for possible fouls on Neymar and Gabriel Jesus, but both times the referee waved away their protests.

With 76 minutes on the clock, and time running out for Brazil, Coutinho drifted in from the left flank with the ball at his feet.

He spotted the run of Renato Augusto through the centre, and played a delightful chip over the defender's head and into Augusto's path.

Augusto met the ball perfectly with his head, and planted the ball past Courtois.

2-1.

Brazil had finally beaten the Belgium keeper.

Now in the ascendancy, Brazil were eager to restart quickly, to keep up the momentum.

Soon after the kick-off, Neymar darted down the left wing, chasing a loose ball. He cut the ball back for Coutinho, but his shot failed to hit the target.

In this half, Brazil had enjoyed most of the possession,

and had taken three times as many shots as Belgium. But still, they couldn't get back on level terms.

As the clock ticked down into stoppage time, Douglas Costa went on a mazy dribble for Brazil, before prodding the ball to Neymar on the edge of the area.

The whole stadium seemed to hold its breath. At this moment, there was nobody Brazil would rather have on the ball than Neymar.

He struck the ball first time, fizzing it towards the top corner. At the last moment, Courtois leapt, and somehow managed to get his fingertips to the ball, flicking it over the bar. There was no way past him.

When the final whistle went, moments later, Neymar sunk to his knees.

Once again, his World Cup dream was over.

17
AGONY

August 2020, Estádio da Luz, Lisbon, Portugal
Champions League Final, PSG v Bayern Munich

"It's been a strange year," the PSG manager, Thomas Tuchel, told his players. "And the game today won't be any less strange. There'll be no fans in the stadium – so, when the going gets tough, we'll have to inspire each other. And it will get tough – have no doubt about that. Bayern are a very good team."

Neymar had struggled with anxiety during the

COVID pandemic, as had many other people. He'd been isolating in his home, keeping as far away from the pandemic as he could.

In the end, he was grateful that nobody from his family had suffered from the disease. But the uncertainty had been difficult for him to deal with, not knowing when – or whether – life would go back to normal.

All football had stopped for more than four months, as the world adjusted to the new reality. And then, even when football had returned, the crowds had not – and the stadiums had been left eerily quiet.

PSG had actually done well over the course of the season, once again winning the Ligue 1 title, as well as winning the finals of the Coupe de France and Coupe de la Ligue.

And now they were in the Champions League final – for the first time in their history.

After the last-16, the knockout stages of the tournament had been played in a special format, with all games taking place behind closed doors in Lisbon.

So far in the tournament, PSG had demonstrated exactly why they were considered one of the best teams in the world. They'd narrowly beaten Dortmund, and then Atalanta in the early stages, before cruising past RB Leipzig in the semi-finals, with a comfortable 3-0 win.

They were now within touching distance of the biggest prize in European football.

"Yeah, Bayern are OK – but we're not a bad team either, boss!" Neymar called out, trying to lighten the mood in the dressing room.

"That's the spirit. Let's give everyone back home something to celebrate!" added Thiago Silva, the PSG captain, as the players got ready to walk out onto the pitch.

As they made their way down the tunnel, the reality of Tuchel's words sank in. The stadium was empty. Neymar would normally be greeted by the energy and the roars of the crowd, but today, only the players' voices echoed around the 60,000 empty seats.

The players weren't even allowed to line up alongside their opponents, owing to the COVID distancing regulations, so Bayern were made to walk out behind the PSG players.

As Thomas Tuchel had made clear, Bayern were a very good team. They had won a clean sweep of domestic trophies, and their squad featured top players such as Robert Lewandowski, the dangerous Polish striker.

All of the context faded away as the match kicked off. This was the one big trophy that Neymar wanted to win for PSG. It was the project he had joined PSG for – to win the biggest trophies and to write history for a club with a blank slate, where he would be the star player.

Neymar did have one challenger for the title of undisputed star of PSG, though. Kylian Mbappé had joined PSG three weeks after Neymar, for a fee of up to 180 million euros, making him the second most expensive player of all time – after Neymar, of course.

The first ten minutes of the game were cagey, with each team finding their rhythm. Without the encouragement of the fans, momentum was proving harder to build.

After 17 minutes, PSG – and Neymar – had their first chance. Mbappé picked the ball up on the left wing, before laying it inside the Bayern full-back for Neymar to chase. Neymar struck it first time, but the Bayern keeper, Manuel Neuer, managed to get a hand to the ball and divert it behind.

Just a few minutes later, Lewandowski had his first sight of goal for Bayern. He swivelled on the ball and unleashed a fearsome strike, which cannoned back off the PSG post.

"That was your warning!" Tuchel called out from the sidelines, urging his players to stay focused.

For the rest of the first half, both sides continued to trade chances, but neither team could break the deadlock.

Then, fifteen minutes into the second half, Bayern's Joshua Kimmich exchanged passes with Serge Gnabry on the right wing, before curling the ball towards the far post.

Kingsley Coman met the ball and planted a firm header past PSG keeper Keylor Navas.

Bayern had the lead – and it was an ex-PSG player, Paris-born Kingsley Coman, who had come back to haunt them.

Coman ran to celebrate at the corner flag with his

team-mates – and their cheers echoed around the empty stands.

"Come on, lads!" called out Thiago Silva, trying to encourage the PSG players. "If we had fans here, you know they'd be getting behind us. Ney! We might need some more of your magic tonight," he added.

The PSG players tried to respond to going behind. Mbappé had a penalty appeal turned down, after his ankle was clipped in the area and then, when he did finally find himself free in the Bayern box, he was flagged offside.

The minutes ticked away, and the shouts from the PSG players became more frantic.

As their star signing, Neymar felt particularly responsible, but he just couldn't find a way through.

Then, a minute into stoppage time, Neymar got his chance. Mbappé received the ball on the edge of the area, doing a couple of step-overs to pull the defenders out of position, before sliding the ball through to Neymar.

Neymar span on the ball, before firing it across the goal, towards the far post. A number of PSG players tried to reach it, but nobody could provide the finishing touch. The ball rolled agonisingly wide of the goal.

Minutes later, it was all over.

PSG had lost the Champions League to Bayern.

Neymar was devastated. All the emotions he'd bottled up over the last few months came out – emotions he didn't even realise he'd been keeping down.

Another player came over and hugged him, and Neymar was surprised when he looked up to see David Alaba, the Bayern Munich defender, standing in front of him.

"Congratulations," Neymar said weakly.

"I know you have a lot of pressure on your shoulders, Ney. You carry the whole club. You deserved to win today," Alaba said quietly, before turning to rejoin his team-mates.

18
FRIENDS REUNITED

August 2021, Camp des Loges training ground, Paris, France

"Is it too soon to joke about it?" Messi asked Neymar with a grin.

Neymar just raised an eyebrow and kept jogging.

Messi had arrived at the Paris Saint-Germain training ground that morning, for his first training session with the club.

He'd arrived two hours early, and by the time Neymar

had arrived, Messi had already introduced himself to the rest of the squad.

The two old friends had embraced. "You were a big part of why I wanted to come here, you know," Messi had told him. "Neither of us have won the Champions League since we won it together, at Barca."

"Getting the old gang back together!" Neymar smiled.

"Except, instead of Suárez, this time we have Donatello ... " Neymar added, looking over at Kylian Mbappé. There was a slight resemblance to the cartoon character, which was how Mbappé had acquired the nickname.

"Oi! Don't make me embarrass you in front of your friend, old man!" called out Mbappé.

When the day's training started, Messi immediately showed his quality – even at 34 years of age.

The ball seemed to be drawn to his feet, as if it was magnetised. He would flick the ball up, higher and higher, but could always catch it perfectly on his instep.

Neymar sensed the competitive spirit rising in him. He wanted to show his friend what he could do – and do it even better.

The pair warmed down together, slowly jogging the length of the pitch. The last time they had met each other had been at the Copa América in Brazil, just a month earlier. Neither player had ever won this trophy – and that had been an oversight they had both wanted to rectify.

They'd both started in equally electric fashion. Neymar had scored twice, as Brazil had easily topped their group, remaining unbeaten.

Argentina had matched their results, with Messi scoring three times.

Brazil had squeezed through the quarter and semi-finals, winning each game 1-0. Argentina had comfortably won their quarter-final, with Messi scoring – before he'd then scored the winning penalty in their semi-final shootout.

So Brazil had been set to meet Argentina in the final. Now either Neymar or Messi had been guaranteed to break their hoodoo and win a senior trophy with their national team.

Before the final, the Player of the Tournament winner had been announced and, for the first time ever, two players would share the award – Messi and Neymar.

It had seemed perfectly fitting.

The final had been at the Maracanã, where Neymar had experienced so much joy and heartache.

This time, it had been more heartache, as Messi's Argentina had won 1-0 to take the title.

And now Messi was at PSG. Despite everything he'd said, Neymar knew that Messi would really have preferred to stay at Barcelona. He was only moving because of the club's financial problems.

But if Messi had to go anywhere, Neymar was glad that he'd come to PSG.

Four years ago, when Neymar had left Barcelona, he'd wanted, above all, to be his new club's star player.

But he'd begun to realise that the only way to win trophies, whether for the club or individually, was by having the best players around him.

Neymar thought back to tournaments he'd played when he was young, when his father would have to explain to him why he hadn't been winning, even though he'd been the best player on the pitch.

Now, Neymar was ready to win – as part of a team that contained the very best players.

19
LEGEND

December 2022, Education City Stadium, Al Rayyan, Qatar
World Cup Quarter-Final, Brazil v Croatia

It was Neymar's third World Cup – and his third World Cup quarter-final. He had never played a game deeper into the competition.

Brazil had only made it past the quarter-finals once since 2002, and that had been the 7-1 semi-final defeat against Germany in 2014. Neymar had been out injured for that game – and was happy to forget all about it.

This time, Neymar was sure, it would all be different.

He'd come into this World Cup at the age of 30. He'd been playing for his country for 12 years now, and only Cafu, Roberto Carlos and Dani Alves had ever played more times for Brazil.

But Neymar wasn't interested in appearance stats. He cared about goals. And it was the Brazil goal record that he was hunting.

He'd come into this tournament with 75 goals for his country – an amazing achievement for any player. He'd long passed heroes of Brazil such as Ronaldo, Romário and Zico. His target now was the legendary Pelé, who'd retired on 77 goals. Neymar needed just two goals to equal his hero's record.

Brazil had reached the quarter-final stage fairly comfortably. Neymar had started in Brazil's first group game, but had gone off injured with a sprained ankle.

He'd immediately feared that his World Cup would be over due to injury, just as in 2014. But the doctors had reassured him that he'd only need a couple of weeks to recover. If Brazil made it to the knockouts, he'd be fit to play in them.

In fact, Neymar had returned to play against South Korea, in the round of 16, and he'd scored a goal in their 4-1 win, putting him just one goal behind Pelé's record.

Neymar walked slowly out into the stadium, alongside his long-time PSG team-mates, Thiago Silva and Marquinhos. Brazil were meeting Croatia in the quarter-final – a canny and hugely talented team, too easy to underestimate.

In the middle of the pitch there stood a huge replica of the World Cup trophy. Not wanting to think too far ahead, Neymar didn't dare look at it. There were still three games between him and the trophy – he just needed to focus on each game in turn.

"I'd appreciate it if you could win this one for me, please, Ney," said Thiago Silva. "I don't think I've got many World Cups left in me."

"Yeah, 38 is pretty old … " replied Neymar. "I'll see what I can do. Got to respect your elders."

"Hey, don't forget about me!" Dani Alves called from the touchline. "I'm even older than Thiago!"

Neymar laughed, grateful to have a distraction from the big game ahead.

Neymar was aware of his own age too. Thiago Silva and Dani Alves were defenders, and defenders playing into their mid-thirties wasn't uncommon. But Neymar was a forward, and he would be 34 at the next World Cup. Perhaps this would be his last chance as well.

The game started slowly, with neither team wanting to make a mistake. Ivan Perišić had an early chance for Croatia, scuffing a shot narrowly past the far post.

Then, shortly afterwards, Brazil's Vinícius Júnior played a dangerous one-two on the edge of the area, but his shot couldn't beat the Croatia keeper.

The rest of the first half was a cagey affair, with neither side breaking through. So far, both teams had played as cautiously as possible.

As the players came out of the dressing room for the second half, Neymar was aware that he had just 45 minutes – to get the goal to equal Pelés record, and to send Brazil through to the first World Cup semi-final that he would be able to play in.

The second half was a more frantic affair. Neymar

had an early chance, shooting on the swivel, but his shot was charged down by the Croatia defenders.

Then he was played through on the left-hand side of the area but, this time, it was the keeper who blocked his shot.

Minutes later, Neymar broke through the defence and had another attempt at goal – but again it was saved, this time by the trailing leg of the keeper.

The 90 minutes finished at 0-0. It was going to take extra-time to separate the two sides.

Neymar could sense the tension amongst his team-mates, as they prepared for another 30 minutes. They were already physically and emotionally drained.

Neymar, on the other hand, was energised. He had another half an hour to score his record-equalling goal and he knew that, if he dug deep, he'd be able to beat the tired Croatia players.

It took until the 105th minute for him to get another chance. Neymar dropped deep to get the ball from Marquinhos, before playing a quick one-two with Rodrygo, as he approached the penalty area.

He slid the ball into the feet of Lucas Paquetá on the

edge of the area, receiving the ball back, surrounded by Croatia defenders.

Neymar danced around the defenders, shrugging them off as he approached the keeper. He jinked one way, sending the keeper to the floor then, from a tight angle rocketed the ball into the roof of the net.

"GOAL!" he shouted wildly.

This goal meant more to him than any that had come before in his career. He ran towards the corner flag, thumping the Brazil badge on his shirt, before pumping his fist in the air in ecstasy.

In that moment, as his team-mates smothered him, he thought back to the little boy, gazing in awe in the Santos museum. He remembered feeling starstruck, looking at the memorabilia of Pelé – O Rei, The King. And now, here he was, the kid from Mogi das Cruzes, equalling the legendary Pelé's goal record, on the biggest stage of them all.

And Neymar knew one thing, for sure.

He wasn't finished yet.

HOW MANY HAVE YOU READ?

MESSI	KELLY	HAALAND	RONALDO	SALAH
PULISIC	KANE	NEYMAR	MBAPPÉ	SON
SAKA	LEWANDOWSKI	FÉLIX	GNABRY	STERLING
RASHFORD	KANTÉ	SILVA	VAN DIJK	MAHREZ
SANCHO	KLOPP	SOUTHGATE	GUARDIOLA	